God Speaks to Us in
Feeding Stories

Bible Stories Adapted by
Mary Ann Getty-Sullivan

Illustrated by
Marygrace Dulski Antkowski

God Gives Bread from Heaven

Exodus 16:3-36

The People of God set out for the Promised Land and left Egypt behind. Many doubted that they would be taken care of in the desert like God had promised them. After only a little while, they began to complain and to be angry with Moses and Aaron and their sister Miriam.

The people wondered if they had made a mistake to leave Egypt. They said to one another: "At least in Egypt we had salad everyday; we had food to eat and houses to live in, even if we were treated badly."

They began to believe that, although they were slaves in Egypt, it was better there than in the desert where they were not sure of anything, even of how or when they would eat. In the desert they had to learn to trust God. It was hard for them to believe what Moses said about all the wonderful things God would do for them.

God knew exactly what they were thinking. So it was no surprise when Moses and his brother Aaron came to God to ask what they should tell the people. God said, "I will rain down bread from heaven for you. Everyday the people are to go out and gather their daily portion of the bread I will send. On the sixth day, however, they shall bring in twice as much as they gather the other days.

"The seventh day is the Sabbath, a day of complete rest. It is sacred to the Lord. You will need to show that you trust me on this day. On the Sabbath, no one will gather any manna. On the seventh day you will eat what you have gathered on the sixth day. You are to rest and to remember my words on the Lord's day."

The people were still grumbling about leaving Egypt when Moses and Aaron returned and told them that God would send them bread from heaven. But the people still wondered how they could have bread from heaven. They spent the whole day and evening complaining.

But the next morning, when the people got up, they saw that God had spoken truly. On the ground was dew which evaporated and became like bread, good to eat. They tasted it, and it was sweet, like honey. Moses instructed them to gather just enough for their families, one day at a time. Many worried that there would not be any the next day. They thought they should gather more than they needed and save it in case there wouldn't be any tomorrow. But they soon found out that Moses was speaking for God. When they tried to gather too much and to save it secretly, the honey-bread from heaven, called manna, was spoiled the next day. They had to learn to trust God to give them the daily bread each new day.

So each morning new manna appeared, enough to go around and satisfy everyone—for one day only. But on the sixth day, there was enough for everyone to last two days. Then, on the seventh day there was no manna to gather. This was the only day that manna saved from the day before was not spoiled. No manna fell from heaven the seventh day. On the seventh day, the Sabbath, the people ate manna that had been gathered on the sixth day. And they remembered God's words.

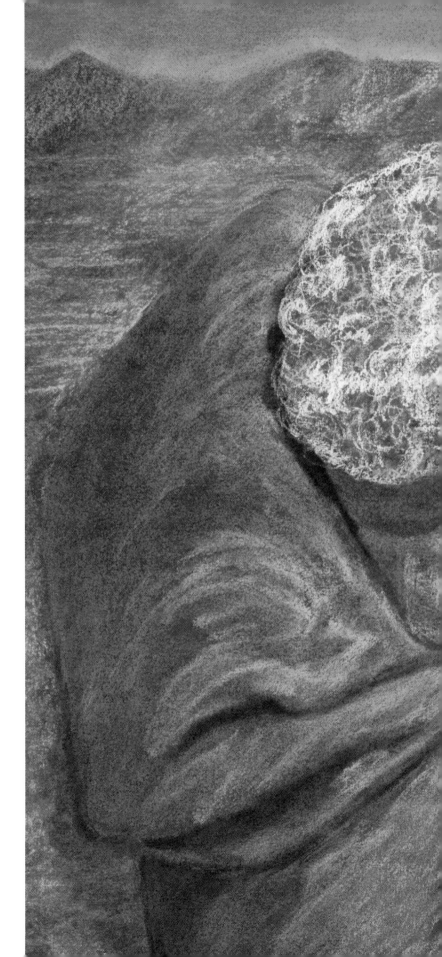

The people had their daily bread and more. Every evening, meat in the form of quail came and was there for the people to eat. Evening and morning, each day, God fed the people. They learned to depend on God and to trust God. They learned that what God had done for them yesterday and today, God would do again for them tomorrow. Each day they had what they needed and they knew it came from God.

GOD SPEAKS TO US THIS FEEDING STORY about how the people had food to eat for forty years as they followed Moses and Aaron, living in the desert and learning to trust God.

David and the Holy Bread

1 Samuel 21:2-8

David was the great king of Israel. David came after Saul, the first king. Before David was made king, he worked for Saul. He had many duties. He was an armor bearer. David was a fine musician who played beautiful music that soothed and comforted Saul, the king.

Once David went on a long journey, accompanied by many soldiers. They had to leave quickly, and there was no time to pack food. So after they were on the road awhile, they became hungry, and they wondered where they could get some bread.

David had an idea. He went to the priest and asked for food. David asked, "Please give us five loaves of bread or however much you have on hand."

The priest hesitated just a moment. He told David, "I have no ordinary bread to offer, but only bread that has been blessed, called shewbread. It is God's bread, holy bread. Therefore you and the others must be blessed in order to eat it."

David replied, "We are blessed. God will surely be pleased to share the bread with us." So David and all the others had bread to eat that day, and they knew that this bread was from God. They ate the holy bread, and they gave thanks to God who did not let them go hungry.

AND SO GOD SPEAKS TO US THIS FEEDING STORY, reminding us that bread is a blessing, a sign of God's care for us.

God Feeds Elijah, the Woman, and Her Child

1 Kings 17:1–18:3; 2 Kings 1:9

There was a very holy man, a friend of God, named Elijah. Elijah lived in the desert very simply from what God provided in nature. Even the clothes Elijah wore came from the world around him. He wore clothing made of animal hair and skin, and a leather belt. Elijah often prayed in the desert, and everyone knew that he was very close to God.

God often spoke to Elijah, and Elijah always listened to God. Once God told Elijah, "Go and inform King Ahad of Israel that there will be a drought on the land. For a very long time it will not rain. There will not even be dew on the grass in the morning. It will only rain again when I tell you. Then everyone will know that Elijah speaks the word of God." Elijah did as he was told and informed the king of Israel that no rain would fall until God said it would.

And so it happened that there was no rain at all in the land. A bitter famine accompanied the drought. There was no food and no water in the land. But God told Elijah where there was a stream of water, and Elijah found it as God said. God sent birds called ravens to bring food to Elijah beside the stream. So even though there was no water or food in the rest of the land, God took care of Elijah.

After some time, however, that stream dried up, too. God then said to Elijah, "Go now to a far place, and I will take care of you there. I will see to it that a poor woman feeds you."

Elijah did whatever God told him to do. He went to a strange city, and there he saw a poor woman gathering kindling wood. Elijah asked her for a drink of water. Just as the woman was going to get the water, Elijah asked for some food to eat. The woman responded, "Sir, I have no food except a little bit of flour, just enough to make a loaf of bread for myself and for my little son. I am going to heat the last of the water and make the bread, and that will be all we will have." Elijah said, "All right; do as you say. But share the little loaf with me, too. And God will take care of all three of us." Neither the woman nor Elijah knew how there would be enough.

25

But the woman was courageous and generous. She shared the little she had with Elijah. Then Elijah said, "I have another word from God to speak with you. God promises that there will be enough flour and oil and water for us until it rains again." And the woman and her son and Elijah had enough food and water to live on for another year, until it rained again. This is what God had promised, and it came true.

AND SO GOD SPEAKS TO US THIS FEEDING STORY, reminding us that sharing what we have pleases God who watches over us and gives us what we need.

God Sends Elisha to Feed the Crowd

2 Kings 2:9-13; 4:42-44

Elisha was a young man and a great friend of Elijah. Now Elijah was growing old. One day Elisha asked his friend for a very special gift. "Elijah, please give me a double portion of your spirit so that I may be able to carry on your work. You are growing tired. I will be able to help you if I have your spirit." Elijah answered his young friend: "You do not know how difficult this could be for you. Your request is up to God. If you are here to see me taken up from you, you will know that God has granted your request. You will have a sign."

28

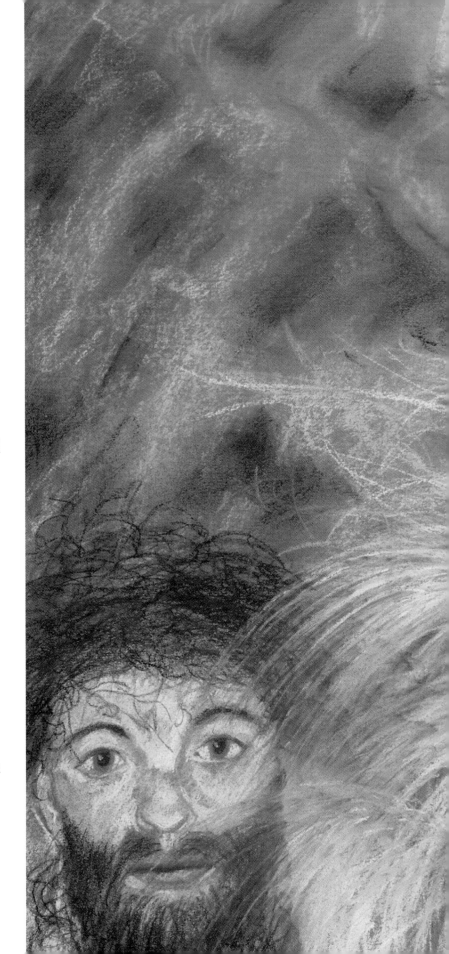

While they were walking along and speaking heart-to-heart, a fiery chariot came for Elijah. Elijah jumped into the chariot and was taken off to heaven to be with God. Elisha saw this happen. Then suddenly Elijah's cloak, the one he had used when he performed miracles, floated down from the sky where Elijah had been taken up. Elisha ran to pick it up. He knew that this was the sign he was hoping for. Having this cloak meant that Elisha now could do the same things that Elijah had done. Elisha was also a prophet, like Elijah. Elisha spoke only the words that God told Elisha to speak. These words were the power of God to make great and wonderful things come true.

Then one day Elisha was speaking to many people, more than a hundred. A man brought Elisha twenty loaves of bread, made fresh with the finest ingredients. Elisha was hungry, but he did not immediately take some for himself. Instead he said to the man, "Please give this to all the people."

"But," the man objected, "how can this little food feed so many, more than a hundred?" Elisha answered, "I speak God's word. They shall all eat, and some will still be left over." And when they had eaten, there was some left over, just like God said through Elisha the prophet.

AND SO GOD SPEAKS TO US THIS FEEDING STORY, reminding us that in every age there are prophets given to care for us and to tell us what is right to do.

Jesus Changes Water into Wine

John 2:1-12

Once there was a wedding, and Jesus' mother and Jesus and his friends were all invited. It was a large celebration. And in those days especially, people celebrated with wine. Now a lot of wine had been ordered for the party, but still it ran out. Mary, Jesus' mother, realized that the families of the bride and groom would be embarrassed if they learned that there was no wine left. As a woman and a mother, she probably noticed such things all the time. So she found her son, Jesus, and said to him, "They have no wine."

At first Jesus seemed not to know what to do. He had not worked any miracles yet and he may have wondered how his mother knew that he could. He said to her, "My hour is not yet come." But Mary knew her son, as mothers do. She told the servants, "Do whatever he tells you to do."

Jesus said to the servants, "I see six large stone jars there. Fill them with water." And the servants did this. Then Jesus said, "Draw out some, take it to the head waiter, and ask him to taste it." The servants knew that they had filled the jars with plain water. They wondered what trick this was. But they did as Mary told them. They did what Jesus asked.

The head waiter was just beginning to realize that the wine was running out, and he was in a panic. The servants brought the water-turned-wine to him and asked him to taste it. The head waiter tasted and then broke into a smile! "I am saved," he thought.

"Someone has been thoughtful enough to save the best wine until last." He did not know the miracle that had been done by Jesus, but the servants and Jesus' mother knew. And they always remembered.

AND SO GOD SPEAKS TO US THIS STORY to help us remember Mary's and Jesus' kindness to us, reminding us that we will have from God all that we really need.

Jesus Feeds the People in the Desert

Matthew 14:13-21; Mark 6:34-44;
Luke 9:10-17; John 6:1-15

People were so happy to be with Jesus because of all the miracles that he did to make them well. But it happened that Jesus became very tired, and he wanted to rest someplace quiet. So Jesus crossed the lake in a boat and ended up on the opposite shore.

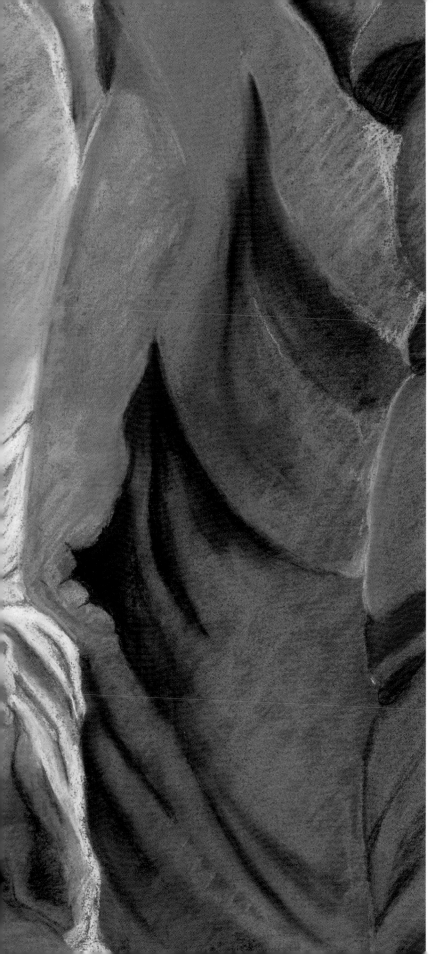

When the people saw that he was going over to the desert, they ran around the lake to meet him. The run made the people very tired and hungry. Jesus forgot that he himself was so tired, and he felt pity for the people. He wanted to feed them.

But his disciples and his friends reminded Jesus that in the desert there are no stores. Jesus already had a better idea anyway. He found out that a little boy had five loaves of bread and two fish.

Jesus knew that the same God who had created the whole world and all that is in it could see what had happened and cared about all the people who were now very hungry. Jesus knew that God was a lot like the mother of the little boy who had packed the food for her son. So Jesus asked God to make lunch for all these children of God out there in the desert.

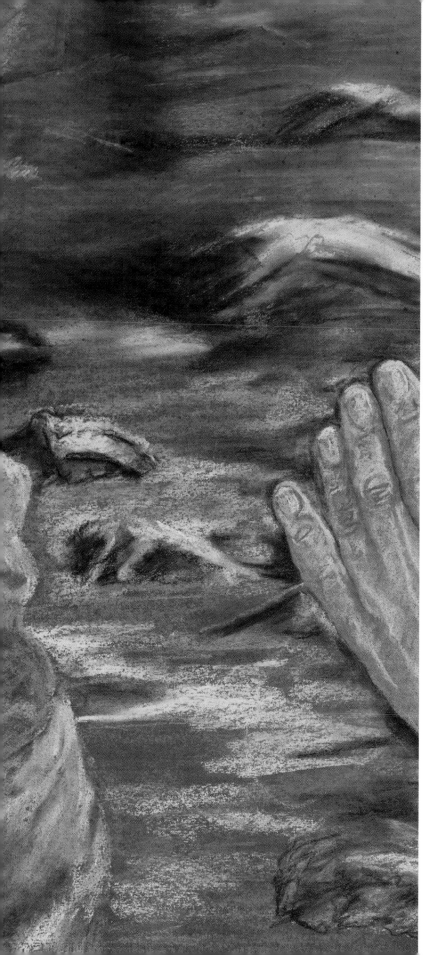

Jesus raised his eyes to heaven to pray. Then he blessed the loaves and the fish, which at first seemed like nothing for thousands of hungry people. But soon everyone had enough to eat. They were happy and relaxed. The disciples of Jesus had distributed the food, and everyone had taken it. Now the disciples went around gathering all the leftovers so that nothing would be wasted. Even at the end, after all the thousands of people had eaten, there still were many baskets of food left over.

So it was that God through Jesus fed five thousand men who were there that day. Of course, the number was more than triple that when the women and children were counted, too. After the people had eaten their fill, they praised God who performed miracles among them through Jesus. The children ran around; full of energy now, they picked flowers in the desert. The adults were content and eager to hear more of Jesus' teachings about the wonderful ways of God.

GOD SPEAKS TO US THIS FEEDING STORY, showing us that our needs will always be taken care of if we rely on God.

The Lord's Supper

*Matthew 26:26-30; Mark 14:12-26;
Luke 22:7-20*

In Jesus' time (and still today), it was the custom to celebrate the great holy day called Passover by eating a meal of lamb and special bread. The people ate this meal in the evening with their families and with their closest friends. It was a most holy feast because then the people remembered what God had done for them, leading them out of the land of slavery.

So, as a remembrance of God's care of them, the people sprinkled blood of a lamb on their doorposts. This was to remind them that they were saved when the angel passed over their houses. So it is that every year the people eat the same food as their fathers and mothers had eaten that first Passover. They eat the lamb and the bread. And they give thanks to God for taking care of them. This is how Jesus also ate the special meal and celebrated the Passover, the holiest of feasts for the Jews.

Now Jesus and his mother and his friends were traveling in Jerusalem, away from home, when the Passover came. Jesus' friends asked him, "Where do you want us to prepare the Passover meal for you and for us?" Jesus answered, "Go into the city, and there you will find someone carrying a jug of water. Follow him and when he gets to his house tell him, 'The Teacher needs a place for the Passover.' He will give you directions, and you must do what he says to do." Jesus' friends did as Jesus said, and it all happened just as Jesus said it would.

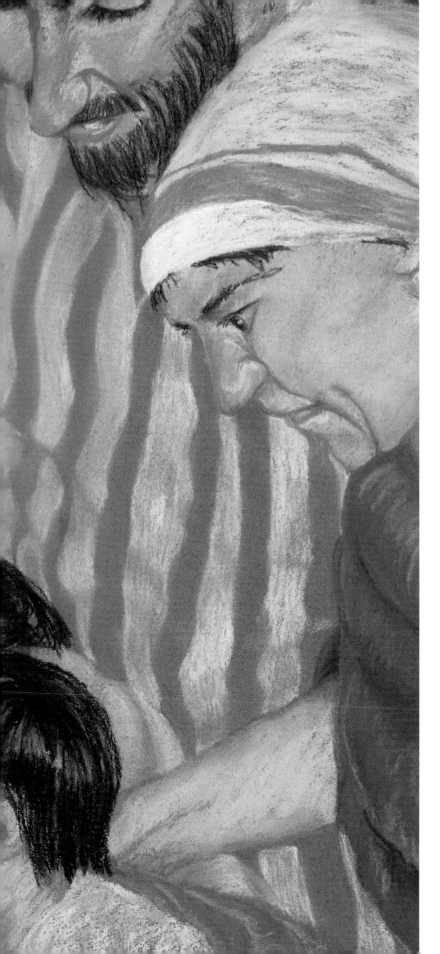

Then when they were eating, Jesus did and said something very important that his friends would always remember. Jesus took the bread in his hands and blessed it. He gave it to his friends and said, "Take this and eat. This is my body which is given for you."

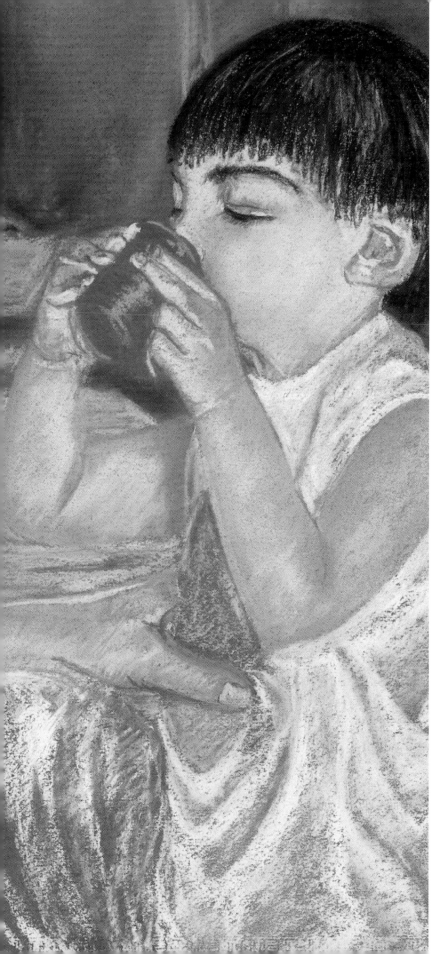

Then Jesus took the cup in his hands. He gave thanks to God, and he gave it to his friends and they all drank. Jesus said to them, "This is the blood of the new covenant which will be shed for many. Do this in memory of me. I shall not eat or drink again with you until we reach the Kingdom of God." And they sang the Passover hymns and then went out to the garden on the opposite hill.

And so whenever Jesus' friends celebrate this night, they remember how Jesus loved them. They remember how Jesus gave them this sign of his love and promised them that he would stay with them through the sharing of this meal.

AND SO GOD SPEAKS TO US THIS FEEDING STORY, giving us a way to celebrate that Jesus remains with us.

Jesus Cooks
for His Friends

John 21:1-4

Once the friends of Jesus were sad because Jesus had gone away. They had no idea when they would see Jesus again. Peter and the others decided to go fishing. After they fished all night and caught nothing, they were tired and hungry.

Jesus was walking along the shore and saw his friends in the boat. He knew that they missed him and that they were tired and hungry and sad. He knew that they had not caught any fish. So Jesus decided to cheer them up. Jesus called out to them to try again. "My friends," Jesus said, "put your nets over the edge of the boat one more time. I think that you will catch some fish after all."

Now Peter and the others still did not know that this was Jesus who was calling to them. Peter was a fisherman and had made a good living out of fishing. He and the others thought that they ought to know how to fish, for they had been working at it a long time. They knew, for example, that they should fish at night and early in the morning when it was still dark. But now it was already light out. It seemed to them that now it was already too late in the day to catch anything. But the idea of trying "one more time" was a good one. After all, the person on the shore might be able to see something that they could not see.

So Peter and the others put their nets out into the water, and immediately the nets were filled to overflowing with fish. When they saw this, they were happy and suddenly did not feel tired at all. They struggled with the fish to bring them into the boat. Now Peter began to suspect something was up. He wondered, "Who is this stranger on the shore?"

Suddenly Peter looked up and realized that the one who had called to them was no stranger. It was Jesus! Jesus always knew how to make Peter happy and when to come to him. Peter told the others, "It is Jesus, the Lord!" And then Peter jumped in the water and swam to the shore to be with Jesus.

And sure enough, Jesus was there. He was already cooking fish for Peter and his friends. Finally everyone else got to the shore. They sat down to eat with Jesus. Now they were all happy and satisfied. They were not tired or hungry or sad, because they were together and Jesus was among them.

SO GOD SPEAKS TO US THIS FEEDING STORY, reminding us that Jesus is always with us, taking care of us and teaching us to trust.

To Dan, one of the clearest ways God speaks to me.
—Mary Ann

With gratitude and love to Michael, my guardian angel.
—Marygrace

A Liturgical Press Book

THE LITURGICAL PRESS
Collegeville, Minnesota

 © 1997 by The Order of St. Benedict, Inc., Collegeville, Minnesota. All rights reserved.

Printed in the United States of America.

1	2	3	4	5	6	7	8	9

Library of Congress Cataloging-in-Publication Data

Getty-Sullivan, Mary Ann, 1943–
    God speaks to us in feeding stories / Bible stories adapted by
Mary Ann Getty-Sullivan ; illustrated by Marygrace Dulski Antkowski.
        p.   cm.
    Summary: Presents stories from both the Old and New Testaments in
which God's power is revealed through food.
    ISBN 0-8146-2365-4
    1. Food in the Bible—Juvenile literature.   2. Miracles—Juvenile
literature.   3. Bible stories, English.   [1. Bible stories.
2. Food in the Bible.]   I. Antkowski, Marygrace Dulski, ill.
II. Title.
BS680.F6G48   1997
220.9'505—dc21   97-14086
                                                         CIP
                                                          AC